YOUR KNOWLEDGE HAS VALUE

- We will publish your bachelor's and
  master's thesis, essays and papers

- Your own eBook and book -
  sold worldwide in all relevant shops

- Earn money with each sale

Upload your text at www.GRIN.com
and publish for free

Kevin Oheix

Yeats, Joyce and Mother Ireland

GRIN Publishing

Bibliographic information published by the German National Library:

The German National Library lists this publication in the National Bibliography; detailed bibliographic data are available on the Internet at http://dnb.dnb.de .

Imprint:

Copyright © 2013 GRIN Verlag GmbH
Print and binding: Books on Demand GmbH, Norderstedt Germany
ISBN: 978-3-656-87795-0

This book at GRIN:

http://www.grin.com/en/e-book/287563/yeats-joyce-and-mother-ireland

GRIN - Your knowledge has value

Since its foundation in 1998, GRIN has specialized in publishing academic texts by students, college teachers and other academics as e-book and printed book. The website www.grin.com is an ideal platform for presenting term papers, final papers, scientific essays, dissertations and specialist books.

Visit us on the internet:

http://www.grin.com/

http://www.facebook.com/grincom

http://www.twitter.com/grin_com

James Joyce and William Butler Yeats are two major figures in modern Irish literature. Both are modernist writers who have experienced the transition through revolutions from Ireland as a colony to Ireland as a Free State and finally as a Republic. Their attitude to narrating the nation and the evolution of their style go hand in hand with the societal and political changes. At that time, there was an intense debate on Ireland's subordination, its relationship with England and its mythologies. This study explores the sort of link which exists between the authors' writings, Irish nationality, and nationalism. To what extent can Joyce and Yeats be said to write about the same Ireland while proceeding in a different way? How do they situate themselves in the process of nation-building? Irish nationalism was much debated during the literary revival up until the Post-Free State period. If it is true that it triggered tensions between those who supported it and those who did not, in the case of Joyce who excluded himself from the native tradition by exiling and Yeats who was static in the invention of a tradition, it is more complex. Both share a cultural memory but also possess their own individual memory in which modernism does not mean the same thing. It will be seen that they participate in the culture they criticize while remaining aloof from it and that the material they use to mount this critique is a form of refuge which at the same time is not directed towards the same goal.

After the flight of the earls and the Famine, Irish culture had deteriorated. Consequently, the Irish politics in the Post-Parnell modern culture of the late nineteenth century was transformed in such a way that nationalistic movements associated with folklore, with its origins in Germany, emerged. The need to shake the ancient Gaelic culture out of its lethargy was expressed through the literary revival led by Patrick Pearse and Douglas Hyde. Their aim was to decolonize and de-anglicize the native country. As colonial and post-colonial writers, Yeats and Joyce had in common a national consciousness. For them like for many, there was a type of Irish thinking. As George Berkeley famously wrote: "We Irish think differently". Literature came to be a medium to express their Otherness as well as their sense of loss. In fact, their essential similarity lies in their criticism and awareness of the conflict between the overwhelming control of the state and the unlimited freedom of the individual. During the conception of the modern nation, it was believed that these forms of tyranny and anarchy could be alleviated. Certainly, the birth of the Free State was a decisive moment in the development of their artistic freedom. Moreover, the censorship act of 1929, marked by anti-intellectualism, had sparked profound reactions from a large number of Irish writers, including Yeats and Joyce. For instance, works such as "*The Countess Cathleen*" and "*Dubliners*" are similar by essence since they are shaped by Irish literary history and culture. Their literature is a literature of process and renewal. Joyce revised *The Sisters* and Yeats rewrote *A Vision*. However, the poet wanted to renew himself in order to be loyal to his art; "It is myself that I remake" (1908), but also to his country. At first sight, one may argue that Yeats is more national and that Joyce is more cosmopolitan. In reality, this is not so evident since their position is ambiguous throughout the history of their country. In the post-colonial period, the Catholic Church was seen as too conventional and very influential with its moral and obscurantist teachings. In a sense, it is no surprise that the Irish society which was then protectionist constantly gave them reasons to resort to a social critique. In their rejection of an objective morality, Walter Pater and William Blake had been influential. In 1937, the period during which the Irish constitution was enacted, Yeats wrote: "I am no Nationalist, except in Ireland for passing reasons". Similarly, Joyce's view as an exile at Trieste was already ambiguous: "Ancient Ireland is dead [...] It is well past time for Ireland to have done once and for all with failure." (1907, *Critical Writings*,, pp.173-4)

For Ireland to achieve this revitalization she had to become modern, yet later in *Ulysses*

(1922) Joyce did not mean that nationalism was the instrument for such modernization. Instead, his modernity, like Yeats's, was accessible to the universal world after independence. In the formation of the modern nation, heteroglossia is an important factor. As Declan Kiberd puts it, "Irish thinkers turned to Europe [...] for ideas and audiences." (161) Indeed, foreign and Irish culture intertwine in the authors' works. Eugene O'Brien notes that Yeats's "earliest poems in *Crossways*, are situated in Arcady, ancient Greece" (118) while James Joyce "located his narratives of Irish life in the [...] Greek mythology" (118) The name Stephen Daedalus in *Ulysses* is an alias indicating a pluralization of the Irish identity which escapes the redundant Ireland/England duality. Fleming writes the following lines on Stephen's geography book:

"Stephen Dedalus is my name,
Ireland is my nation.
Clongowes is my dwelling place
And heaven my expectation." (27)

Here, Irishness is asserted but located elsewhere. Stephen is a resident of the universe who is attracted by other cultures. What is shows is that Joyce was wary of the tyranny of uniformity, he desired to redefine Irishness. In Eugene O'Brien's opinion, the writers achieve this by "'transcending Irish issues" (119) and this is evidenced by their refusal to comply with a narrow vision of nationalism.

An element which links them both as isolated writers is the Irish literary tradition of cyclical history and their experience of violence. Indeed, both sought to appropriate history by rejecting its linear and materialistic view imposed by the imperial state. In *"The Second Coming"* (1921) which dates back to the War of Independence and the partition, Yeats finds out that in his search for identity the individual is left with disorder because he is lacking a stable centre: "Things fall apart; the centre cannot hold; Mere anarchy is loosed upon the world." In other words, an Ireland which tolerates only its own nationality and which is too patriotic is in danger of becoming inconsistent.

The same concern is addressed in *A Portrait of the Artist as a Young Man*. Stephen's emigration comes as a resistance to the uniformity of the revival since his "uncreated conscience" (218) reveals a need to express Irishness from abroad. Joyce wanted to liberate himself from the ideology of history which equates Ireland with Catholic, Gaelic and nationalist opinions. Thus, Stephen asserts that history "is a nightmare from which I am trying to awake" (28) He does not see a heroic past but a linguistic evolution followed by a cultural transformation: "[m]y ancestors threw off their language and took on another" (177)

To a certain extent, the Irish identity is asserted but in an indirect and negative way through the deconstruction of the English language. By using the colonial language from a minor point of view the authors re-envisioned and idealized history. In *A Portrait of the Artist as a Young Man,* Stephen is embarrassed by his language yet his use of the dictionary proves to be powerful against the dean. During the revival, language was politicized in such a way that if one did not speak Irish, one was not Irish. After all, it was the language of history through which a form of revenge for confiscation was made possible. The question of land ownership was directly linked to the linguistic and social realities. Joyce's rebellion against language as the one and only criteria to measure identity takes the form of Hiberno-English which is different from both English and Irish as evidenced by the term "beurla" in *Finnegans Wake* (1939). Yeats also reflects this attitude in his choice to call one of his characters "Paudeen" in his play entitled *The Unicorn from the Stars* (1907). This Hibernicism with its suffix '-een' is indeed an indicator of the hybrid nature of Hiberno-English. As Eugene O'Brien points out, "different languages provide a perspective from whence to mount an immanent critique of one's culture [...]" (215) It is important to add that the reason why the art of Yeats and Joyce is based on legends rather than on history, like the Greeks, is that the Irish history itself is subject to conflicts between tradition and renewal. Indeed, the repressions of the state created in the writers a sense of distance mingled with an obsession with their material which gave rise to the notion of art for art's sake promoted by Oscar Wilde. Both used their culture in order to comment upon it even if that meant returning to the painful origins. Their late style coincides with important shifts in Irish history. Declan Kiberd asserts that "Now that the English have gone, the Irish may draw back from the prosaic quarrel with others to the more poetic quarrel with the self." (319) *A Portrait of the Artist as a Young Man* is more direct than *Dubliners*. Comparatively, Yeats's vision of Irishness became more personal around the revolutionary period and this is evident because the brutal realities of the Revolution were now captured. Aodh De Blacam notes that Yeatsian modernism offers a more realistic approach: "his poetry, […] grew bitter, satiric, and anti-Christian. He [...] wrote in praise of the Ascendancy writers of the eighteenth century, making Berkeley and Swift his masters." (216) Breaking from his devotion to the Old Ireland, he insists in his *"Responsibilities"* (1916) on the distinctiveness between a traditional and a modernist poem. Thus, he discarded his ruritanian themes to deal more particularly with politics. In the same vein, Joyce was uncertain about the future, he preferred to blend the modern with the archaic. As Declan Kiberd points out, "the Irish wished to be modern and counter-modern in one and the same gesture" (330) If it can be said that the intertextuality helps to situate the authors' convergences in their reflections upon nationhood, it also gives a clue to their antagonism. Yeats's late poem *"The Statues"* (1939) is notable in its harsh criticism about the irrelevance of modern Ireland: "We Irish, born into that ancient sect / But thrown upon this filthy modern tide" However, Rosie Partington explains that despite his non-modern intention as evidenced by the content of his poem, "the form which he chooses is undeniably modernist" she adds that "Yeats' desire to retreat to the pre-modern past is unfounded and impossible." which is somewhat reminiscent of T.S Eliot's 'anti-modern modernism.' Ergo, a discussion on the divergences between the two modernists can begin.

As it has been seen, Yeats and Joyce were trying to convey the fluctuations of the Irish experience in a form which could be intelligible to the whole. It will now be argued that Ireland's process of modernization and the nationalist ideology gave rise to unique responses.

Joyce and Yeats introduced their native land in distinct ways. As discussed previously, the desired rebirth of Ancient Ireland and attempts at modernization triggered numerous reactions. In reality, this revival did not imply the same thing for them, it was marked by a sense of heterogeneity. Declan Kiberd suggests that "The real debate of the revivalist generation was about whether the literature it created should be national or cosmopolitan in tone." (156) For Yeats whose invitation to "Sing of old Eire and the ancient ways" in his poem *The Rose* (1893), his literature tended to be national. On the contrary, Joyce did not share the beliefs of the Irish Renaissance as he was unwilling to compromise. What he saw was a redefinition, not an authentic revival. Yeats's National Theatre in the English language represented a contradiction. For the poet, Hiberno-English could indeed revive the Irish past and turn cosmopolitanism into this provincialism which Joyce attacks in his essay *"The Day of The Rabblement"* (1901). To him, the artist should not waste his talent with plays containing uncontemporary legends unknown to the audience. In 1937, Yeats's ambiguity remained: "Gaelic is my national language, but it is not my mother tongue." (*"A General Introduction for My Work"*) As an aristocrat living in London, he was both part of the Irish culture and excluded from it because of his assimilation in British literature. In that regard, Joyce located himself in reaction against his early Pan-Celticism. Seamus Deane insists on "those elements of British culture which he [...] renounced" (12) such as liberalism which he believed was wrong in fueling Irish nationalism. Laurence Davies signals that "Joyce's attitude to the revival was ambiguous" (9) since he used the Irish revivalist themes in order to mock their expectations. For instance, in *A Mother*, his parody of *The Countess Cathleen* with the notion of sacrifice and unity is representative of this antagonistic link between the two Irishmen. Joyce repudiated the idea of a single revival which for him was aloof from the plurality of the contemporary period.

Also, egocentrism is denounced in *A Mother*: "When the Irish Revival began to be appreciable Mrs Kearney determined to take advantage of her daughter's name and brought an Irish teacher to the house." (121) Here, the multiple Dubliners define Irishness in terms of cultural exclusiveness. It seems that for Joyce, the European enthusiasm for the folklore prevents people from considering the Irish economic and linguistic realities. His epiphanies have nothing to do with folklore which he diagnoses as incompatible with modernity because of its non-instinctive nature. In a sense, experimentation with the language allows him to react against the state-imposed revival of the language. As such, Tír na nÓg is derided in *Finnegans Wake*: "or any either world, of Tyre-nan-Og" (24-6).

Social status is yet another essential aspect which divided the authors. Unlike Joyce, Yeats believed in cultural nationalism. His amalgamation of Anglo-Ireland and Gaelic Ireland sought to obliterate the deprivations of the past. Seamus Deane goes as far as to give it a name: "pathology of literary unionism". Through the legends, the aesthete was able to isolate himself from the divisive conflicts of modern Ireland. Born in Sligo, he cared for his homeland and this is noticeable in his depiction of peasantry in the West. The bourgeois world in *Ulysses* was for him something to be abnegated. Joyce was equally contemptuous of the condescending aristocracy that Yeats romanticized. In that sense, Modern Ireland embraces the middle-class culture which *September 1913* rejects and in which O'Leary is glorified: "Romantic Ireland's dead and gone, It's with O'Leary in the grave." The poet, like the novelist, deplores a paralytic society but breaks with the urban Dublin which he considers in *Responsibilities* (1916) as a "place of stone."

Nevertheless, the Dubliner confronted the realities by presenting the paralyzed capital, which Yeats dreaded, to the world. According to Declan Kiberd, he was "alone among the post-colonial writers" because "he did not head for the imperial city or for the lush landscape" (327) In Joyce's opinion, Irishmen were static in their glorification of the Celtic past and therefore unable to forge their own present. Richard Ellman notes that "Joyce's interests embraced parts of Dublin slums, public house – that Yeats found not so much vulgar as irrelevant, he being concerned with monuments or with houses" (476) It can be argued that the poet is traditionalist in his use of the past to assess the present. His political activity and his praise of the historical figures who fought for Ireland are certainly what distinguish him from the revisionist who embraces multiculturalism and emphasizes the corruption. Richard Ellman argues that in Literature, Yeats "raise[d] the ordinary to the heroic" and Joyce "mingled ordinary, heroic, and mock-heroic" (475) For instance, the ancient heroes are present but the traces they left in the Irish landscape are perceived differently. On the one hand, nostalgia prevails in *Easter 1916* with the poet's interrogation on the nature of the rebels' sacrifice to achieve independence: "A terrible beauty is born". On the other hand, disillusionment with the nationalistic politics in *Ivy Day in the Committee Room* is visible in the ridicule of Parnell's successors. As *Easter 1916* confirms, "All changed, changed utterly" and while Parnell's betrayal as well as his failure to give Home Rule to Ireland; "a sow that eats its own farrow", do not evade Joyce in *A Portrait of the Artist as a Young Man*, Yeats sees the founders of the Free State as models and uses rural images to communicate his disappointment about the urban location of the insurrection.

This parochialism is not the only factor which accounts for Yeats's scepticism about European modernity. Considering the fact that Ireland's integration into modernity was done in a violent way, it appeared legitimate for him to remain faithful to the notion of nativism. Joe Cleary notes that "the most embarrassing aspect of the Revival is its folk culture idiom, its nativist or romantic nationalist tones" (221) The dramatist's classical tragedies were therefore politically and culturally ineffective. *The Countess Cathleen* is a primary example of this intellectual paralysis and scepticism since she represents Ireland as an old woman hostile to England's occupation: "too many strangers in the house". On the contrary, modernity was ideal for Joyce in his denial of his Catholic heritage since it was marked by secularization. Rosie Partington suggests that *Dubliners* "are stuck in a cultural no-man's-land, where the violence of colonialism has denied them access to their own course of modernity". Since Ireland was forced to submit to the colonial rule, she could not vie with other advanced nations and this is perhaps why Gabriel Conroy in *The Dead* has decided to spend his holidays in Continental Europe: "I'm sick of my own country, sick of it!" In *"The Second Coming"*, the same idea of stasis is rendered in "the best lack all conviction" thereby revealing Yeats's anti-democratic inclination. Michael Valdez Moses intimates that "Though nationalism itself might be said to be a distinctively modern ideology", Yeats desired "to cultivate an "alternative" form of Irish modernity that was as much at odds with the British imperialism as it was with the [...] official strains of modern Irish nationalism"

In reality, Yeats is a modern representation of the Anglo-Irish Ascendancy tradition and the Big House culture which emerged in the wake of the partition and the Civil War in the 1920s. Neil Corcoran argues that "it finally became plain to Yeats that his dream of an Ireland uniting its best Irish and Anglo-Irish traditions was never to be realized" (33-34) Consequently, he became bitter in *Meditations in Time of Civil War* : "May tilth and loam, Darkened with Celts and Saxons' blood, Breastfeed your love of house and wood" He realized that in the follow-up to the partition, the national identity had been redefined and that even though the Anglo-Irish Protestants were also asserting their Irishness, in the view of Neil Corcoran, a sense of "historical inconclusivenes" remained. However it can be argued that class allegiance, not religion, is what distinguishes Yeats from Joyce. The once senator of the Irish Free State and member of the Irish Republican Brotherhood was more direct in his responsiveness to the political turmoil while the exile turned his back on Gaelic Ireland to reach a sort of neutrality which was ideal for his *non-serviam*. Despite these dissimilitudes, Denis Donoghue concludes that, "the price we pay for Yeats and Joyce is that each in his way gave Irish experience a memorable but narrow definition." (150)

In conclusion, the writers' national consciousness throughout the long transformation of Old Ireland into Modern Ireland has been forged by the contours of imperialist policy and the existing tension between anarchy and order. While their reaction to the colonial discourse is very much the same in terms of a negative definition of Irishness, their response to the challenge raised by the native tradition is singular. As it has been discussed in this study, their work is similar in their originality and hesitation. Moreover, myth and violence affected their narration of the nation in a significant way. They both referred to the same themes such as the revival, the language and the Irish heroes. Each in their own way immortalized the heroes who died for Ireland and assimilated her into British literature but while the poet of the Renaissance utilized the Gaelic culture, Joyce wrote about his country in a more realistic fashion by integrating corrupt characters rather than glorified ones. Furthermore, a poem and a drama are not the same mediums as a short story and a novel. Form and content collide in their works. Yeats is tragic but Joyce is ironic. Despite their divergences, each of their works reveals a concern with modernity and Irish national identity. As the society left behind its repressive past to grow more liberal, secular, and Europeanized, Yeats and Joyce struggled with the concept of Modern Ireland. Certainly, their relationship with her was one of intense debate. In their contestation, they had to find new forms of communication to turn a history of 'shame' into artistic pride and dignity. What they wanted was not so much to reform the components of Irish society as to affirm or reveal the vitality of its people. If for Joyce nationality was not something of high value, Yeats saw identity in terms that were different to the cosmopolitan writer and to the revivalists in general. The short story writer favoured artistic freedom over national culture. In reality, both seemed to fear that after the loss of their native language and culture, their 'great' historical nation was on the threshold of disappearing and therefore its future was uncertain. Even though the two authors possess their divergences about their homeland, they both used literature to express their scepticism and immortalize certain characteristics of Ireland. They saw in art a form of liberation and achievement that the state had failed to guarantee. As both came to be disillusioned with contemporary politics, they realized that Ireland would not meet their expectations neither as an old idealized country nor as a complex modern nation. Finally, what this study has shown is that they must have understood that modernism did not necessarily mean progress. If it is undeniable that Yeats and Joyce transcended nationalism to embrace a universalism, they eventually reached the haunting and perplexing conclusion that the only means by which a nation could attain awareness was through the Other.

Bibliography

Books

CORCORAN, Neil, *After Yeats and Joyce*: *Reading Modern Irish Literature*, Oxford : Oxford University Press, 1997, 195 p

DAVIES, Laurence, Introduction and Notes to *Dubliners*, London : Wordsworth Classics, 2001, 170 p

DE BLACAM, Aodh, *A First Book Of Irish Literature*; *Hiberno-Latin, Gaelic, Anglo-Irish from the earliest times to the present day*, Port Washington, NY : Kennikat Press, 1970, 236 p

DONOGHUE, Denis, *We Irish*: *Essays on Irish Literature and Society*, Berkeley : University of California Press, 1988, 275 p

ELLMAN, Richard, *Yeats and Joyce* : *Being No. XI of the Dolmen Press Yeats Centenary Papers MCMLXV*, Dublin : Dolmen Press, ed Liam Miller, 1967, 479 p

KIBERD, Declan, *Inventing Ireland* : *The Literature of a Modern Nation*, London : Vintage, 1996, 719 p

O'BRIEN, Eugene, *The Question of Irish Identity in The Writings of William Butler Yeats and James Joyce*, New York : Edwin Mellen Press, 1998, 283 p

Articles:

CLEARY, Joe, "Toward a Materialist-Formalist History of Twentieth-Century Irish Literature" in *boundary 2*, Volume 31, Number 1, Spring 2004, 241 p

DEANE, Seamus, "Masked With Matthew Arnold's Face" : Joyce and Liberalism in *The Canadian Journal of Irish Studies*, June 1986, Volume 12, Number 1, 116 p

PARTINGTON, Rosie, "How Have Irish Writers Explored the Relationships Between Modernity, Colonialism, and National Identity?" in *Leading Undergraduate Work in English Studies*, University of Nottingham, Volume 3, 2010-2011, pp. 377-382.

VALDEZ MOSES, Michael, "The Rebirth of Tragedy: Yeats, Nietzsche, the Irish National Theatre, and the Anti-Modern Cult of Cuchulain" in *Modernism/modernity*, Volume 11, Number 3, September 2004, pp 651-579